Karaoke In Da Hood

Karaoke In Da Hood

Traci Gaines

Library of Congress Control Number: 2007909125
ISBN: Hardcover   978-1-4257-9614-3
                  Softcover   978-1-4257-9613-6

This book was printed in the United States of America.

To order additional copies of this book, contact:
Xlibris Corporation
1-888-795-4274
www.Xlibris.com
Orders@Xlibris.com
33691

Acknowledgements

I would like to thank all my karaoke buddies and family for being my inspiration for this book. The names have all been changed to protect the innocent and some not so innocent (smile). This is for you!

Table Of Topics

These are just some of the topics that are discussed in the book. As always I will have a lot more things for people to talk about. There are a lot of things that go on in a karaoke club. Some of the clubs have pool tables. Some of the karaoke places people play dominoes. You'll see some of the regulars and some new people of course. It's just like a friend of mine always says," This is not the Apollo, we just come to sing and have fun."

Foreward

by Traci Gaines

When I first decided to write this story, I decided to write about all of the clubs that I sang karaoke at. At the time I had sang at Ricky's, Shooters, Kimball's Carnival, Rumors, Lucre Lounge, Newark Hilton, End Zone, and the Sports Page. Now I sing at Eli's Mile High Club, the Down Low, the Serenader, and Mels, Bowl. They used to have it also at Crayons, and Hayward Bowl. I didn't get the chance to sing at some of the places because of time and gas prices rising (just bringing that point up on purpose). I wanted to write about all the things that go one at karaoke, and how great it could be if they just give it a try.

Introduction

Karaoke In the Hood is about the different places I've had the pleasure of singing at, and the great friends that I have met. I started out wanting to write about all the fun times I have had at karaoke. Now I'm torn because I have had some friends to turn their back on me. I have sung karaoke for ten years. Don't get me wrong there are some people who really are my friends. For the ones who aren't, the haters, I wish the best in the world for you! I'm going to keep my head up, and keep going strong, and when I make it, I will smile down on you and wave like Princess Di.

Karaoke In Da Hood

My mom used to tell me how great the ghetto was when she was coming up. Boy! has that shit changed! Now at least in my world of karaoke there are a lot of things that were going on that I didn't know about 'til now.

When I first started going to karaoke I loved it. I looked from the audience. There was the KJ, we'll call him Dave. I had ordered a white zin and sat and listened to the music. My home girl Suzie, who had told me to come and see what it was like, told me to pick out a song and sing it. You know me, I'm game, especially when it comes to singin'. I picked out a song wrote it on the slip and handed it to the KJ. He called me up pretty quickly and I sang to my hearts content. Everyone c lapped for me, and then my girl Suzie got up to sing. She tore it up, but as soon as she got back to the table she was saying that she didn't do all that well. My friend and her friend that were waiting their for her had coffee, and her friend had an apple martini.

We were all waiting for the next singer. It was a girl who could not hold a note. She was smiling and having a ball. She was trying to sing one of Natalie Coles' old tunes. Most of us came from the old school days. The next singer was a guy who did his own rap. He used the rappers delight beat but said all his own flow. He was damn good and he knew it. He was looking at all the fine women trying to pick out which one he was gonna get at. When he finished the KJ yelled out, "Alright then dog." We just went on looking for more songs to sing. The KJ had a book full and we were not only trying to remember the songs, but trying to stay sober too.

One of my home girls Jane did not sing at all. I couldn't figure out if she couldn't sing, or was she just too embarassed to get up on stage. I picked out my next song and I could not sing the song worth a damn. I don't know what it was, I had been singing for years, and it just didn't sound right. Besides I was no where near my home girls range. To me, she had the vocal chords of

Gladys Knight or Regina Bell, but she always felt like she didn't sing the song right. Anyway, I cared for a minute, and then I got over it.

When everyone goes to karaoke it is not how you sing, but how much fun you have. Besides if a broad is talking about you, the bitch is probably jealous of what you got or how you sing. Suzie was back up again and this time she sang her favorite song, by Regina Bell. She is in love right now with her babies daddy. She sings like the birds, or God up in heaven is lookin' at her. She can sing loud like the whole world can hear her. It's like she's in a world of her own when she sings that song.

We sang back and forth, the rest of the night. When it was about 12:45p. m., Dave sang the last song. It was a wonderful night, it was a night that I will never forget. The girls and I had a great Girl's Nite Out! When your girl asks you out, you might want to go, you never know how much fun your gonna have.

Now to change back to my usual style. There are a lot of younguns who don't even know most of the artists from the old school. Mariah just made a come back with "The emancipation of Mimi". The album/CD is very good, and another artist is Brian McNight who has, "Find myself in you." You know he has sung for years now and he sounds just as good as always. Even Whitney could come back now but she would have to get with Diddy or somebody to make it again. You know that if it wasn't for Whitney, Luther, Micheal Jackson and many other artists, there would be no videos now. See back in the day the women use to keep there clothes on, like in the Guy videos, Groove Me, and the songs Aaron Hall sang. The Keisha Coles, Guapale, and India Irie are all the new singers now.

For the last two nights I have gone to two great places. On Monday night now we have Apartment C starting again with Bootsy and Veronda. They are very nice Black people, just thought I'd let yall know dat! The food is really good and the music is good too. Pumpkin is the KJ for the apartment. She runs her show well. She has people in order and it's fun. The guys were very gentlemen like, it was cool. Last night we had karaoke at Kimball's Carnival, thankgosh it's free. Vern is the KJ there. I don't get paid until the end of the month. It was nice though. Everyone was dressed. We had a lot of singers, and everyone had fun. Now there was a comment about slobbin' on the mic. Some people just can't help that, so I told everybody slobbin' is good depends on what you doing, that ended that. We have karaoke at Eli's Mile High Club Tonight. Sam is the KJ there, and he has a lot of up to date, and old music. He has some of almost every style.

Now what I've been doing is helping out at Eli's almost everynight depending on what band or venue was there. He has a lot of different things going on. There is metal night with Lava booking. There is Burnin' Bush night with Kim and Trina. Venus Fly Love is another night. Partying/Karaoke with Jason, and Dancing to old school with Chris. There is a night of Blues with Billy and The Thrillers. They also have a jam session with Dean on Sundays! Eli's always has a calendar at the door. So far karaoke is every wednesday and thursday for the month of September.

I currently work all the time for the high school. I also go to Ricky's for the evening and write my books. Then I go to Eli's, Serenader, Shooter's, The sports page, The Down Low, Kimball's Carnival, The Lucre Lounge, Mel's Bowl. This is my eleventh year now. I have had a ball over the years. So many friends I have met along the way, sorry to say and lost.

I had the chance to go to L.A. and I rode first class on Amtrak. I wanted my friend and I to go to final drafts' movie script conference. The dates were 4/20-4/22, 2007. We left on Thursday the 19th in the morning and the guy we had was great. I had salmon on the first night. The car is actually very comfortable, and it has two sides on the bottom. That part is seats. There is a bed on top. The seats also let down to a bed. When we were able to go to dinner, we had to sit in the dining cart. There was a car in between where people could sit and watch the view. It was wonderful! It took eight hours for us to get to L.A.

The view was wonderful to, I actually was able to do a video with my phone along the way. When we got to LA, Jay D's cousin picked us up from the train station. Then he took us to the parking lot near the hotel. We had to walk up the hill to get to the main entrance. The entrance looked so good after that walk. When we got to the room it was nice. We settled in and eventually went to sleep. The next morning we had to be at the conference for ten. We got our badges, they had our names and the bronze package typed on the front. We went to the restaurant and ordered breakfast. It was good and our waiter was very nice. I love to go to a restaurant and the service is good. I told the manager how good he really was. Then we went back up to the conference. The seminars were Never use your own money, battle scars; Storytelling; A Laugh A Minute; the Big Picture; Thinking Outside The Box-Office; Scare Tactics; Element Of Surprise-Plot Twists; Finding Financing; Animation; creating emotions And Game; Women Who Kick Ass(you know I loves this one!), and protect yourself. The directors that I met personally were Wes and Johnathan Craven, Jessica Bendinger, Simon Kinberg, Carl Ellsworth, Steven Susco, and Antwone Fisher. I went up to Antwone Fisher and introduced myself and then handed him my bussiness cards for my books. The director that sat next to him said, "Yeah, that's what I'm talking about. Jessica Bendinger was so nice, she thanked me for coming and sitting in the front. I told her thankyou for speaking at the conference. One of the directors even came to sit in at the seminar the next day. We had a total of three days. One of the guys that made the program for Final Draft, gave me some tips, and menus to look for and also emailing for help. I told him that I definetly needed that, and that I would write about the conference in my book. I have trading cards with all of the directors, background information on them. They all had block buster movies. The rest of the directors are Hank Nelken, Stephanie Allain, Bruce Evans and Raynold Gideon, Andrea Berloff, Chris Morgan, Kevin Smith, Syd Field, Diana Ossana, Peter Iliff, Jon Crowly, and Bobby Moresco. I feel they were all great! They had the chance to work on some great films!

On February 2, 2007 I was able to start working for Channel 2. I went in right after work. So most of my days went from 3:30 until 11p.m. I had a ball! I would get the scripts ready for the 5 and 6 O'clock news. I was able to work with and meet Mark Ibanez, Sarah Sidner, Bill Martin, Amir, Ellen, Janice, Carma, Bonnevie, Marcus, Julie Haener, Ken Wayne, Mike Mibach, Monique, Dennis Richmond, The crew from Traffic,. We had three seminars while I was there newswriting, safety(in a new truck), and anchoring. I had the pleasure of working with before he retired. They gave him a going away party and he was on the news that last evening. Then Dave took his place, he's was fast, thorough, and great! I would always tell him, "That's A Wrap" when the last script was given to the anchoring team. I made me feel like I was sort of working in film too, which is a living dream of mine.

Ever since July 12, 2007, I have made six videos to try and be Diddy's personal Assistant! I write almost everyday, just trying to get things off of my chest! Diddy makes videos every now and then telling us about how it is to be his personal assistant! In the mean time I still go on day to day trying to get out there, stronger and stronger. Here are some of the messages I sent!

My professor said that I could do the homework and then finish the paper. I'm glad. I have to type up one page when I get off of here. I have to ask my class mate if she can bring the work next Wednesday. I am feeling really hot right now. I didn't go to work today. I will go on Monday. I haven't felt good, mostly tired but I have noticed to that I'm eating later and later. I haven't eaten for today yet. I think I will go to Subway for myself and mom later. My friend the bar manager wants me to help her with her garage sell. She wants to get up at 6 in the morning. I told her that I would spend the night. I have five time sheets for Berkeley. I hope they pay me on time. Next 15th something should be in the bank. the woman at the union asked if I worked 50 days yet. I told her that I don't think so. I am going to count soon. I have worked 21 days. Everything is half way. My Die Hard Raider Fans Book is half way now.

I want to finish it before the season is over. That may be the one to send me to stardom. There are a lot of Raiderfans. It's RAIDERNATION Baby! I love that. I will get back into gear come Monday. I told my class mate that now I am just going to school and working for the Districts, but I feel so funny not multi-tasking. I have noticed though that I don't count writing you everyday. Blogging and Bulletin writing, up the but. My page on tvproducing is full of my blogs. It's my birthday on November 18th. Maybe I'll get a prince charming to fly his jet out to Oakland, say hi, and then go back to his work! I should put that in a book. That would be messed up, but it's better than nothing at all. I know I'm Crazy but I say it's a good Crazy. I am ready to get something sometime. I have some money that I was saving. Lunch is all that I can think of. I have a friend that is performing at a local club on Saturday. She said that I wasn't coming. I am so tired. I think I'll surprise her and show up after resting behind the garage sell. Oh my gosh, there's soldier girl with that you, you you in it. That part cracks me up, but I think they were genius the way they came back to back like that. I just wonder how long he's going to last. Now instead of one hit wonders they have one week wonders! I still say where is Genuine! I heard him on the radio last night singing my pony. I was going to write a blog about it, but I'll give everybody a break for a while! my B-Day is November 18th. I am a Scorpio! Yes I do fit the bill, if it's a baller! I'm just kidding. I am sort of saving myself now! I'm just so busy that I can't get with no one. The next time I'm in a car it better be worth it. I just imagined, the car in your song with Mario would be great! Ok I'm getting to close now! Especially to someone I hardly talk to. I told you I was getting hot! Ok I've got to go now! I'm looking at hell date now! It is so funny! I just saw you on 106 and park, "This is beautiful," and you dancing. You are so handsome! Oh my gosh it's pizza hut now. It's 2:28 and the only thing I have to do now is go to Eli's. I want to look at a whole bunch of different movies. I let my professor look at two of my movies yesterday. I have to pay for distribution for my dvd/documentary! I really should go in there and get some of that roasted chicken and some potato salad. Guys kill me with a girl that is negativity. She is not going to be happy all the time. Like you, and your serious video. Me, and the bar manager were talking about that last night. People at karaoke want me to be happy all the time. I feel if I'm happy than they feel better. I want to be happy with going from state to state doing my book signings. Paying for a higher priced package so that I can do that. I can't wait to say to everyone, I'm going to New York, then Paris, and then Japan. That reminds me, a friend is moving to LA. I told her good luck and we will miss her. She said she's not looking for fame. I told her that I will look for it until the day that I die. I noticed you said that you haven't made it yet. Oh my gosh Diddy! I know how you feel though. I haven't gotten to where I've wanted to. I will talk to you sometime tonight. I'll let you know how tomorrow goes too. It's blues tonight. I'm happy Traci

I am freezing my butt off, here at the garage sale. There are a lot of Latino families. I get to practice some of my Spanish now. I like speaking it, but I don't feel comfortable. I don't mind sitting here though! I have more patience than the law allows. I wonder sometimes. I can't write too long because I am trying to help out! I will talk to you soon! Traci have a great day!

THERE ARE A LOT OF THINGS I HAVE TO DO WHEN I GET HOME. I HAVE TO GET WITH THE WORK FROM THE MOVIE. I HAVE TO GET WITH MY CHAPTERS FROM MY MASTERS! I HAVE A LOT TO DO! i WILL TALK TO YOU WHEN I GET THE CHANCE! TRACI

I had tenth grade science students all day today. The teacher had them watching a movie on meteorites. The security guard said that she would be gone for a few days. I wonder where they're going to put me tomorrow. I will talk to you tomorrow most likely. I am not going to sing tonight. I have my books to read. I will catch up more maybe later. if I just so happen to wake up later which I know I will. Have a great evening! Traci

Well I'm still waking up for the times of being at karaoke, but I gotta slow down. I still need to work on school. I also have to work on work. At San Leandro I want to see where my time sheet is today. I have four days as of today. I will find out in just a few minutes. I will talk to you after work. I can get on the internet, but the mouse won't work with the Myspace page. Hayward is calling now. I'm at San Leandro until friday! Have a great day! Traci

All that talking that my friend does about the Lakers. The first thing he's gonna say, "Pre-season." But I'm gonna make a blog just for him. He talks so much shit! There in the fourth quarter with 8:52 to go. It's 12:05, Barnes got the fowl,from the warriors. The Lakers are caught up almost. It's GS 93,LAL 91. Maybe I won't send him a blog(ha ha). I know guys don't care about how close you came, it's who wins the game. It'a now a tie game. Wow, the Warriors were 17 points ahead. Lakers 95 for the first time. The warriors missed the basket. Now it's tied again at 95. 5:51 left, Wow that's why basketball is so much fun. They take you back and forth, all through the game. Your emotions go up and down, and then there's the end. I just pictured your peeing video for a second. That is so crazy of you!(ha ha) Warriors up 3,lakers 2. Now Barnes travels! That's not good towards the end. Hudson is fouled. La up by one with 99.Azubuike misses the first free throw, gets the second, game tied at 99. GS in the lead with 101. Crittenton fouled, makes both, game tied at 101. It's

3:27 remaining. LAL 104, and a three point lead. It's Azubuike to the line again, he misses both, that's why they sent him to the line. 2:46 and it will be warriors ball. I just figured it out, I am going to copy and paste some of these to the desk top and save them in a folder, so I can type it up later. Like the notes on the warriors game can go into my Die Hard Raider Fans Book. They are in Hawaii, I plan to go there, at the Stan Sheriff Center. It's GS 103,LA 104. GS 105,Lal 106. They fouled Azubuike again, yay he got the first one and the second one, it's 107 to 106 Lal. Hudson hits great free throws, it's GA 109 and Lal 106. Lal 108 and GS 109. Lal has 109 at the free throw line, with one more free throw left. Lal 110 now and Warriors 109. Warriors have the ball with ten seconds to go. Now 4 seconds to go and the warriors have the final timeout. Hudson got it for the win. Troy Hudson," Welcome to the warriors," the announcer says. It was 112 GS to Lal 110. they changed it to a two point shot, It's 111 GS to 110 Lal. Lakers try to lob it and misses. The warriors win the game,Yay! Go Warriors! Any way I guess I'll have to pull it up again and retype it. It will always be in my sent folder. 2 million being taken back from Micheal Vick! Oh my gosh, leave him alone! It's raining out here to. Joe Torry may be dismissed. They say George Steinbrenner wants to make a change. So good night, and I will talk to you tomorrow. I have to go to sleep. It's 12:48, and I will be up in between a few times. Traci

All I have to do is copy it to a word document· Now I need to look through the rest of them, to try and get this book done. It's a lot of info that I wrote to you about, and I should've been writing it in one of my books. I want to get these next two out, so I can go on to the next one. I will talk to you tomorrow. I have a lot to think about. Traci

I didn't have a subbing assignment today. I sat from 8a.m. until now 2:14 OR 2:00 typing. I turned on the car and I heard voices, I though I heard Mike so I kept listening! I said to myself I bet that's them. Then they got into the conversation about the show. Then towards the end they were talking about who they wanted to work with. Then they talked about the girls they wanted to meet at the show. Then they sang a little. They sounded good. Sana and the crew put on Hood Nigga, and I jumped out the car. I have to finish typing up the notes from the Movie. I finished all my home work thankgosh. I got up to chapter three in the typing I'm supposed to do for the Black Panther Party Movie. I decided to come in and write you first. I'm at Ricky's until time to go to Hayward. I will leave at about 5. I'm only around the corner now. I will talk to you later, I've got a lot more typing to do. Traci

All I have to do is copy it to a word document· Now I need to look through the rest of them, to try and get this book done. It's a lot of info that

I wrote to you about, and I should've been writing it in one of my books. I want to get these next two out, so I can go on to the next one. I will talk to you tomorrow. I have a lot to think about. Traci

After class at Hayward, I went to karaoke! I am soooooo tired. I will talk to you in the morning. I am out! Traci

This is when the alarm goes off! I usually hit it until about 7:30 now, but the secretary told me, or the sub coordinator told me that she will need me tomorrow. I'm typing with my eyes part open. The rain is pouring down. B5 was on Kmel in the morning when I went to work. i tried to call Chewy and tell him to play he song again. He's so stupid, he played part of the song and said, "Ok you want to hear the rest of the song go and get the CD." The nurses are on strike at Alta Bates Hospital here in Oakland. A boy has been strangled and poisoned and they feel it's been by his mother. They were filming by Berkeley high. It's 6:37, a homicide in Hayward. My mom wants me to go back to Channel 2, but I can't right now. I think about it, but I'm concentrating on this Masters now. We go t film in Oakland for the movie on Tuesday. The woman I work with has pride in me now because of typing the ten chapters—notes-in one day. I love it. The owner of the bar Ricky's got mad at me because I said when I become a full fledged star, walking on the red carpet in my diamond studded dress, people could kiss my but, the ones who don't believe me. I told her yes, I'm being mean, but everyone just don't know how it feels to be right at the age, workin'(grindin'), and what's happening, at least what I want, is not happening yet. I hate the fact that everything is going so slow. She isn't a people person either. She asked me why was I interested in see and talking to everyone one on Myspace! I told her that I love that too, I'm a people person. She asks about you all the time, and wonders have you made a decision. A fourteen year old had 40 weapons with a book on how to use them. The teen was planning a Columbine attack on a middle school. He was bullied! Police are investigating the parents. The mom will be arrested for buying the boy a gun. he will be accused of possibly making a terrorist threat, and having weapons. Jena six member jailed for 18 months. Accused of beating a white student. EA's boo million dollar purchase! Stocks, I called a stock company who only took in a million at a time! I told the woman, I am going to get to the amount, and would like to know how to get into the stock market. 880 66th accident, right by my house, but I don't take the freeway. That's the only thing that's convenient with San Leandro, I can drive right down Bancroft, and get to work. I love it. After I get through typing for the movie, I have to type on the Die Hard Raider Fans and finish it. I'm going to call the book company today, and see how far I have to go. I wrote it down before but I want to make the dead live my Birthday! November 18th, so that I can hsve three things to celebrate. Making 40(shh,don't tell noboady yet), even though I look like late twenties, Singing karaoke for ten years, and finishing at least one of the books, if not both. Chocolate may have a biologic effect. Help obesity, change bacteria in the, something? A new India Jones by Speilberg. Filmed in Fresno. I would love to be able to work with him, or for him. I have to make the three million dollar movie that I want. I've sent the script to two places now. I have one other company. That reminds me! I've thought about your email again. I know you sent it to me, I received the list confirmation. I saved the address in my email. I just want to hear from you, and was hoping you had a personal email address, but I know you can't know me yet. I am very loyal, I usually stay friends with someone for years. I am going with a friend that I've known from karaoke for ten years, to a play. Whatever she wants, at the paramount, with Vivica Fox. The nurses are headed into the Hospital. Now it's mornings on two with Tory, she went to my College. She's cool on TV, but she's not very friendly in person. I hate that, the only way I would be mean as a star, is if someone was mean to me, just before, but maybe not. I have been pissed off at not being paid, or something and still treated the kids fine. i will be going to San Leandro soon. I will talk to you later on, or later tonight. My usual schedule. I have to go to work, then come home. I have to get to the play for 8:00pm. I told my friend if I had the funds we would go in a limo. The next play I will. Then the manager told me well after the play maybe you could come sing. So I'll be dropping into Eli's after the play. I'm use to this though. It's been cool for a while now, because the boys say that kids always approach them saying, your Ms. Gaines' son. They say adults do too. A woman put her hand up for money getting on the bus, or shuttle. The hospital signed a five day contract with replacement nurses. California Nurses Association will take action if the nurses will not be allowed back into the hospitals. A guy hit a girl in San Jose, then tried to sexually molest her. What movie was he watching. Beckman looks so young, and had dramatically tried to change his appearance. The market will plan to charge for parking meters. Depending on the area, they will charge what they want. So in the rich areas it will be 5 dollars to park at a meter. Anyway, I have to get dressed. I will talk to you later. Traci

I'm with the advanced kids! They have done their work early. I called my book company and told them that I will have the die hard finished by my birthday Nov 18. I will have it done then. I will talk to you from Ricky's I'm going to type for a while afterwards before going to the play! I hope it's not ten times for this code today Traci

I WILL TALK TO YOU SOON. I AM AT RICKY'S AND THEN AT ABOUT TO GO TO THE PLAY THAT I WROTE MY BLOG ON. WHATEVER SHE WANTS. I WILL TALK TO YOU LATER. THE PLAY I'M GOING TO ELI'S MILE HIGH CLUB TO SING! I SANG FOR THE KIDS TODAY IN CLASS. THEY GET A BIG KICK OUT OF IT. IT TOOK ME FIVE TIMES TO GET THROUGH THE SECURITY WITH MY SIDEKICK. THE STUDENTS TOLD ME THAT IT DEPENDS ON WHERE YOU HAVE RECEPTION. ALLRIGHT I'M GONE. TRACI

I am tired. I went to Eli's after the play. I met Boris only because he was the only one to come out for pics. It's 3:24am. I will do the blog tomorrow! Good night, sleep tight don't let the bed bugs bite! I can't even type right(that rhymes ha ha)! Traci

I tried to click to see what my Diddy IQ was? It didn't work. I'll try again later. I want to get paid from Berkeley so I've been talking with the union. I still have two days that their supposed to pay me for. I want my money. I have to read a lot this week so, I think I'm going to take off tomorrow. We will be filming and making B-Roll tomorrow. The woman I work with, said as long as it's not raining. I will be with them working. I want to get some rest today. I have to read my homework. I am halfway in the Raiders book now. People in bands are asking to be in my karaoke in Da Hood Book. I just figured that I would do that anyway. Now I just realized that I might as well mention all the groups that you have on your bulletins, or send a message saying like, if there's a new group. For right now I will mention B5,Gorilla Zoe, Making The band 3(?)(It's 4, I had to be sleepy), Young Joc, and if there's anyone, oh yeah, my girls Danity kane, Cherie Dennis, Cassie. I can't think of anymore right now, I'm sleepy. I went to Denny's and ate, also picked up mom some breakfast. I bought NBA Live 08 for my psp. I will talk to you later. I have to get some rest. My stomach was hurting earlier like I had the flu. Now It's ok. Traci

I ADDED ON CASSIE! I WENT TO ADD BAD BOY BLOG! THAT'S HOW I CAN REMEMBER ALL THE GROUPS! I AM SO SLEEPY! MY STOMACH IS KILLING ME. IT'S BEEN HURTING FOR TWO DAYS NOW. E NEWS IS ON NOW! THE ONLY REASON WE LOOK AT THESE IS TO GET A CHANCE TO SEE THE STARS. I WILL NOW DEAL WITH AS MANY THINGS AS POSSIBLE BEFORE THIS WEEK IS OVER! WHEN I'M NOT DOING A LOT,THERE'S NOT MUCH TO WRITE. I WILL BE ABLE TO SEE IF, WE'RE GOING TO SHOOT(FILM) IN A FEW HOURS.

IT'S 8:22AM. I CALLED THE WOMAN THAT I WORK WITH! I TOLD HER THAT IT'S NICE AND SUNNY! I WANT TO WORK ON

THE FILM LOCATIONS TODAY! I WILL TRY AND GO TO WORK
TOMORROW! I AM STILL HAVING STOMACH PROBLEMS. IT'S
ACTUALLY MAKING ME LOOK LIKE I'VE WORKED OUT. I WILL
LET YOU NO HOW THE SHOOTING TURNS OUT! I HOPE IT'S
GREAT. IF IT ALL COMES DOWN TO IT, SHE WANTED TO WORK
ON THURSDAY. I WANT TO GET IT OVER WITH TODAY. A GUY
WAS TAJEN INTO ARREST FOR STABBIN' EX-GIRLFRIEND THAT
WAS IN COLLEGE. I'M WATCHING MSNBC NOW! HE STABBED
HER NEAR THE LOBBY, NEAR A SERVICE AREA. HYDROCHOLORIC
ACID IS COMING FROM A COMPANY IN MICHIGAN. IT'S OUTSIDE
OF DETROIT. THEY SAY IF IT RAINS IT WILL MAKE A CHEMICAL
CLOUD. JUST GOT THE CALL, MAYBE WE'LL DO IT ON THURSDAY!
I'M GLAD I DON'T RELY ON THIS STUFF EMOTIONALLY I WOULD
BE SO HURT RIGHT NOW. SHE SAYS THAT SHE HAS TO FINISH
ONE OF HER OTHER PROJECTS BY TODAY. I HAVE TO CRANK
OUT MY READING TODAY FROM SCHOOL. I DON'T KNOW
IF I MENTIONED IT BUT I RECEIVED THE LETTER FROM DR.
MURHY AT CAL STATE EASTBAY. THERE ARE 24 CLASSES THAT ARE
NEEDED TO WAVE THE ENGLISH CSET(CALIFORNIA SUBJECT
EXAM FOR TEACHERS). I HAVE EIGHT THAT QUALIFIED. THERE
ARE 16 THAT I HAVE TO DO. I WAS TOLD THAT IT HAS TO BE
BY JANUARY 2008! WELL I HAVE TO TAKE THE TES THEN. I HAD
PLANNED ON TAKING IT ONCE TO SEE WHAT IT WAS LIKE. WHEN
THOSE PEOPLE TAKE ALL THOSE CLASSES, THEY ARE THEN OVER
QUALIFIED FOR THAT TEST. I HAVE A GUT FEELING. IF WE ARE
TAKING THOSE TESTS THEN WE ARE DOING WELL. I'VE HAD
TO TAKE THE MULTISUBJECT TWICE SO FAR! I GOT VERY CLOSE
TO PASSING. THE MULTISUBJECT TEST IS FOR EVERY SUBJECT
AND FOR GRADES K-6(ELEMENTARY) I KNOW SOME TEACHERS
THEY LET WORK IN THE MIDDLE SCHOOLS WITH THE MULTI
SUBJECT BEHIND THEM, BUT THEY WERE TELLING THEM THAT
THEY HAD TO PASS THE SINGLE SUBJECT IF THEY WANTED TO
KEEP THEIR JOBS(I WON'T SAY WHAT DISTRICT THAT WAS). IF I
CAN GET PAST THE TEST I CAN STILL GO INTO THE CREDENTIAL
PROGRAM, AND FINALLY MAKE IT TO FULL FLEDGED TEACHER,
ALL THE TIME, UNLESS I GET TO WORK FOR YOU, AND THEN
LEAVE INTO A NEW LIFE. NOW THEY HAVE REPUBLICANS VS.
REPUBLICANS! I WILL TALK TO YOU LATER OR SOMETHING!
MY STOMACH REALLY HURTS. I AM THINKING ABOUT EATING,

BUT I DON'T WANT TO GAIN A LOT OF WEIGHT. I WANT TO MAYBE GET SOMETHING FOR ME AND MOM, BUT I'LL FIGURE IT OUT! I MAY SEND MY SON TO GET IT! I TOLD MY YOUNGEST SON, THAT I NEED TO GET THEM AN OUTFIT, AND WE GO TO A STUDIO. WE NEED TO TAKE SOME UP TO DATE PICS FOR MYSPACE. I DIDN'T TAKE MY BUSINESS CARDS TO THE MOVIES YESTERDAY EITHER. I HAD A BALLL WATCHING TYLER PERRY'S WHY DID I GET MARRIED. OF COURSE BECAUSE IT HAD MY GIRL IN IT(JANET), BUT IT WAS DAMN GOOD. I'VE ALREADY LEARNED FROM PLENTY OF WOMAN THAT THERE IS ALWAYS BETTER OUT THERE. YOU JUST HAVE TO FIND THAT PERSON. I WANT ONE DAY ONE OF THOSE FAIRY TALE WEDDINGS LIKE ON TV, BUT I NEVER REALIZED THAT I COULD GET THAT FROM BEING AN ACTRESS. YOU CAN BEST BELIEVE THAT I'M GOING TO APPEAR IN MY OWN MOVIES LIKE SPEILBERG, AND WHO EVER ELSE. I'M DREAMING AGAIN. HAVE A GREAT DAY DIDDY! I'LL TALK TO YOU!

I didn't ask her her name, or if she has graduated already, but she was with her girlfriend in an escalade! I told her as long as she was doing what she had set out to do in life, that's what I was happy about! Her friend had told me that she was ashamed. I told her that because I know what it was like growing up and I used to get into places before I was twenty one. I'm glad I'm going on—looking like twenty. My friend said it's the way I danced. Tonight he wouldn't have guessed that. My life has worked out different than I wanted it to. that's why I admire you! I have watched you over the years and I still want to be like Diddy! I want to work for you so bad to proove that having a degree means something! I am going for my masters as long as they will keep me in the program. If I graduate it's only because of my gift if gab, and my hard work that it happens. I want to work with you to see if my dream that if you are working poor which I learned from Hayward, will still get you to being rich will work. I'm not a bad person, and I must admit I don't want your money. I want to have money just like you! Diddy I'm being serious here! If you had known me way before this you would have known! I am only contacting all of the stars because I want to be like you all! Not to take advantage! I will work very hard for you! I will have your back regardless what happens! it's 1:24am and I am typing to let you know about all this. I think you are very handsome but if you didn't think that I am qualified, I still have to keep going! I will go to work at one of the districts tomorrow and then I have to go to class tomorrow and Thursday. I am actually going to another class on Thursday to finish up an incomplete grade! I always have to do make up work. It's only because I didn't want to have some of my classmates help me before but now I have no choice. I am going to keep going with my masters until they tell me I can't go no more! Then I'll have to do like my bachelors, appeal, and then receive it anyway! I want to be like you, with the billions in dollars only because I think that's the answer from being working poor! My friend told me at one point that I was middle class! I haven't gotten there yet! I'm not ashamed I have worked my ass off for what I have now. I have all my accomplishments, plus going for your personal assistant! I know that I have the brains to do it! The lifting is a whole other story, but If I could join a fitness place like my older son! I was up to 90 pounds with nautilus before! I would look just like Janet! as far as weight goes! I had a ball tonight though! I sang and came home! I got on the computer and then I'm going to have to type that damn long security code to send you this damn message! I gotta like you to do that on a daily basis anyway! Inuasha is on now and I'm sleepy! It's 1:34am, goodnight, sleep tight! Traci

I've known for a very long time! I used to exercise once a day! Now I'm doing all this silly stuff and lazy in between. Wow, I just noticed that my friends who are on line, I can send a message too. Myspace is amazing. My stomach has been hurting since Friday. I'm tired of being in the house, I'm going to Eli's soon. I have to go and shoot on location tomorrow. The lady I'm working with said that she would come by at ten. I told her to come on. I guess I'll go back to work on Monday. I have had two weeks vacation! I'll be cryin' later. Now I know what it would be like just staying at home and taking care of mom though! It would drive me nuts to be in the house like this! I want to move! I have been here for two long now! I want to go and see Brazil, unless Gorilla Zoe was just talking. I do want to see other places. I have been in Oakland all my life! I've been listening to the hypnotist that's been on Montell. "Power" that's what he teaches. He's at sylver.com. He says very positive words, and hypnotizes you into believing that your a millionaire! of course you don't need this, but the audio stream can relax you after a stressful day! There's a guy that looked at my Myspace pics and said did you gain weight since I first saw you! I told him, no I'm still the same weight as when he first met me! I don't go up or down, my weight stays stagnate(?). It's the clothes that I wear that make me look big, big. Every time I tell someone how big I am they say no way. I'm 5'5 1/2, and I have a chest that's 40, a waste that's ok, and a butt that's 42 maybe. I haven't measured myself in a long time. My male friends say I'm just thick. They say there are a lot of women that are way bigger than myself. I just want to get some new things going on. I guess I'll head to the club now! Traci

I just saw the children video! I thought it was cute, that you called it home alone! Jocs on rappin' brown paper bag! I feel like superwoman. I'm sitting here in my t-shirt, and Raiders undies. I feel hotter than all get out! 106 and park is on now. It's Thursday Oct 18,Roxy says. We had fun riding all over Oakland. When I was looking at Keyshia Coles new video, I thought of an idea. I wonder if you can do a B5, Joc, or Da Band video where there are three girls at home watching their videos on the computer. There were four of us all looking at the video at the same time. I'm gonna go and Common got his first award for his CD! That's good. I am so tired, but wired, and I'm trying not to think about Eli's but I only have a little while. Oh yeah, I just remember I bought a cranberry juice, and two waters that are owed to me. I think I will go. I just love singing so much. I know if I danced more, I would lose some of this weight too. Anyway, I've taken the shirt off now. Kanye rapped, I'm good. I love that song. He gave his award to big boy, and common for the video. They say big boy, gave it back. Good night man! I'll talk to you tomorrow! Oh yeah the woman that I work with, said, yeah, that's what makes you a good assistant producer. Oh yeah, I'm glad you have the pool pic. You should take another one for me right by those waters where the water is see through, and that pretty blue! Like I say travel for me, until I can grow up, and be just like you Diddy! there's a friend of mine who has a daughter that is getting straight a's in school! She's trying to convince her to go to Howard1 I told her with the A's and wanting to go into Nursing, that's a great combo! I had to touch your pic on the computer, those abs are so scrumptious! I always laugh when I see that pic. I hope you take some pics at the parties, If I could fly out, I would take them. I have to get ready for next week. It's back to work, and school. I know it's the most important. I went this morning to pick up my moms meds at Kaiser. I keep trying to tell her that we have to get her the mailing program that they have. I then went to my favorite breakfast place and ate. I had the bacon, grits, eggs over easy, and white toast. I then went to get breakfast for mom and my oldest son. I am trying to make my meals one a day. I know I like the liquid drinking. I knew that would take the weight down. I haven't been able to get my hair done lately. that always happens. I'm so busy taking care of everything else that I can't do the pretty stuff for myself. Let alone, like you say cocoa butter skin, and Toni Braxton with her milk baths, or is that Mariah. It may be both, hell. I want to be pampered too. I'm going to though! When I get my next funds I'm going on a trip or treating myself to an expensive hotel. That's how I reward myself. I still haven't done the spa treatments yet. I'm working on all that though. I am going to go and figure out how to paste all these messages I sent to you!, chop em up, and get this book done of mine. Karaoke in Da Hood is going to be finished. I got a rejection email from Benderspink. that's another film company that I sent the script to. It's ok though! Like I said before, whether you hire me as the personal assistant or not(I would love the job) I gotta keep going! Have a great day, Diddy! I hope everything is going well for you, and that God is giving you all the blessings that you hope for and more! Traci

I have been on here since 2hrs and fifteen minutes. The making the band 4 video had my oldest son singing. He even said that he wants to take voice lessons. I think for a young man, he sings pretty good. Of course cause he got it from me! My youngest is more into rappin. He's in my song on my Myspace page. I let most of the kids here it in school they say they like it! the don't get mad at me one! He's the one at the last verse. Call me the future . . . I sort of laughed because his phrases had to come from me going to college and talking to him all the time. My mom taught me proper English, so I taught it to them. It has helped me a lot along the way! Sometimes I feel like a white girl in a black girls body! It's all good though! I just want to get away! I want to be able to travel too! ANYWAY HAVE A GOOD ONE! TRACI

I am very grateful to Tom and Myspace! Here are some of the blogs that I've written! When I get the chance I will make it to a club near you and take photos and write a story! I love to write! I love to take Pics! I love to hang around the beautiful people! I mean everyone in this world!

Wednesday, October 18, 2006

I want to know are there any good men out there?
Current mood: bitchy
Category: angry *Quiz/Survey*

I have been around some great men. I have been around some serious players. i want to know how women or men feel about players. There are a lot of men friends that I have, and they have great manners. They walk me to my car when we go out. They have great conversation. Some of my friends take me to romantic places. I really want proof that there are more men out there for the Black women in America. I know that men say women can be players too. Men of the world let me know how you feel about a women that's a player. I was told by one person that this subject can be negative. How would you feel if someone just continued to step on your heart, even though you tried to be a good women. A person can only take so much. As far as my culture, I feel the men need to step up and change their game. Like I always say, "If it's not you, It's all good." Granted I can proudly say that is really great! I must say that I love the men that are true gentlemen! Tell me what you think everyone! Traci

Wednesday, December 20, 2006

brittany,the girls, and miss usa
Current mood: annoyed
Category: *Movies, TV, Celebrities*

Donald has decided to keep Tara as Miss USA. On one channel the title on the screen read Trump keeps the tramp, or something like that. She supposedly was doing crack, and she kissed miss teen usa. The only part I'm paying attention to is the going out. Will you people please tell me how you feel about a woman going out all the time. I have two teens who are almost done with high school. I go to sing karaoke a lot of nights out of the week. what is wrong with a woman going out all of the time! I have wanted to sing all my life. I have one song that is done. Roll-X from heat lab studios composed the music, and I wrote all the lyrics. We're currently working on 8 more songs. I have taken voice classes at state, and the university level. I have even had private lessons before. What is wrong with men going out all the time and it's ok? When women go out their wh—? Tell me what you think?

Sunday, December 24, 2006

dating!what do you ask for in a guy?
Current mood: curious
Category: *Romance and Relationships*

I ask for going to the movies. I like to go out to dinner. I like to travel. I like going to plays. Is this telling too much information? I have grown up in an old fashion way, and I feel you shouldn't have to tell a guy to do anything. I feel they should give gifts on their own. People say not to look for a guy, they say let him find you. They say that a woman will not meet the right guy in a club at all. They say that all women should know that, but every woman I talk to says she needs a good guy that will marry her. Then there are some women who claim they can be by themselves. Tell mw ht you all think!

Thursday, December 28, 2006

When your out shopping have you had a good experience or not?
Current mood: annoyed
Category: *Fashion, Style, Shopping*

I have had the greatest time in shopping lately. The attitude of a salesman or sales woman is very important to me. If I have a bad experience I will not patronize that store anymore. If I have a good experience then I buy, and may go back for years. If I have a bad experience, then they may never see me again. What has happened to all of you? Did you go through a bad experience? Did you go through a good experience?

Thursday, January 04, 2007

Do you believe in NewYears Resolutions?
Current mood: busy
Category: *Quiz/Survey*

I didn't make any resolutions for New Years. I used to always write them down and work hard at keeping them. I have put my foot down on some issues though. I vow to be by myself for the next year. I will definitely work on more movies. I will work on my masters and my career. I was able to meet Joe Torry the comedian for the New Year. Mt friend gave myself and a friend, tickets to the Comedy show at the skybox. Sheryl Underwood and the host were great. They were all good. Happy New Year everybody! Traci

Monday, January 22, 2007

Do dreams really come true!
Current mood: jubilant
Category: *Goals, Plans, Hopes*

I just recently met someone, who can help me find the way, to the future that I've always wanted. We met just by chance. I chose to eat breakfast, and he chose to come and get breakfast. I can now work with a music video production company. Everyone says keep dreaming! Don't give up on your dreams! I say it was nothing but God! I know everyone has their spiritual preference. What are your dreams and have you achieved, or received them? I say that God creates all kinds of little miracles, you just have to look for them. Well I hope that everyone in this world, gets the wishes of their lifetime! Traci

Monday, February 19, 2007

Why do they call women crazy!
Current mood: aggravated
Category: *Romance and Relationships*

Why is crazy the best word for women now, when men are just as crazy? I hate it when they say oh she's crazy. Women have a lot of different situations goin' on in there lives. Let alone the men in there lives calling them crazy. Men have a lot of issues, and I feel that they have periods, they just don't bleed. Men gossip with each other all the time. If their not talking about women sexually, then it's sports or something else. I want to know from the women and the men out there, why can't everybody get along?

9:30 AM—2 Comments—0 Kudos—Add Comment—Edit—Remove

How does it feel when you've lost the love of your life!
Current mood: confused
Category: *Romance and Relationships*

I recently have decided to call it quits with a guy who I've been around for eleven years. I have had friends to tell me leave him alone. I have left him alone and as soon as he calls, I go running back. I know that we had problems. I know we had things we didn't agree on. I am so out done from all the changes I tried to make in myself, but I'm supposed to be the problem. I want to let all women know that you are a queen within yourself. No matter what a guy tells you, you love yourself the most. Even if he tells you that you are the problem, you're not. I told him that it was both of us, we are the problem. I feel very good about myself. I know I am a great person. I want to find a person that can love me just the way I am. I want that person to love me with all there heart. I want us to be able to conversate about anything and everything. I want to be with that person and just have a good time. Let me know how your heart has been broken, and how did you fix it!

Friday, March 23, 2007

Why is it so hard to lose weight or easy to gain weight!
Current mood: apathetic
Category: *Food and Restaurants*

I know during the summer I ate a lot of junk. I ate a lot at Jack, Mickey, Wend, Kent, and a few other places. Just last year I lost forty pounds. A friend of mine told me don't get too skinny. Now I feel like I'm a fat pig. Some of the guys tell me I have all the weight in the right places. I know that it's not healthy. I eat a lot more fruits and vegetables. I have even taken Hoodia to lose weight. I didn't think it was working. My friend told me it was a suppressant. It worked though. I don't eat as much. I finished it a few weeks ago. I feel a lot better. My face is getting slimmer. I can't fit into my old jeans yet but I'm sure something will happen soon. I want to lose the weight and keep it off, like the commercial says! Tell me your stories about losing or gaining weight and if it's been hard or not. Traci

Friday, March 23, 2007

Men are bitches and have periods too!
Current mood: bitchy

Sometimes don't you want to say to your man, you actin' like a Bitch! Sometimes they get to fussin' and there's nothing you can say to them. They go on and on just like a woman. Oh my gosh, you almost wanna Bitch Slap Em! I know someone who said that the guy she knows has his period the same time she does. He gets moody right around her last three days. I remember when friends of mine used to get angry when I became angry. I remember them just going off on me for no reason. When they would calm down, then they would apologize. It's amazing the way they can turn their feelings off and on. they can treat you like shit, and then turn around like they did nothing at all. I wonder what it is like to be in there shoes? Tell me your stories about the men you know! Traci

Friday, March 30, 2007

How do you guys handle a budget? Can you or Can't you?
Current mood: aggravated
Category: *Goals, Plans, Hopes*

I am now trying to start a budget. I can finally be comfortable in my own skin, but I want to make it safe. I don't have a mint yet! I want to be comfortable like some of my friends. I know that it takes discipline. I know that it takes planning and hard work. I want to buy everything under the sun. I keep telling myself that I need something else. I know that I have a lot of things under the sun. I know that I have enough clothes to wear. I know that I have enough shoes to wear. Let me know how you feel about budgeting and whether you like it or not. Let me know how you budget your money, or if you are able to at all. I know that some people can't budget because they don't have much! Sometimes you might be broke right after you get paid. You might be broke before you get paid. let me know how you handle things. Traci

Friday, April 06, 2007

How do you handle being tense at the job? Is it fate?
Current mood: busy
Category: *Jobs, Work, Careers*

I had a little tension from a reaction, after getting a certain reaction from my boss. I know that you stress out at the job. I know that you have to get over it. It will pass once you and the person talk. How do you guys handle stress, or someone chewing you out? How do you handle someone talking to you like your lower than thou? What do you do when someone literally looks at you like your crazy? Do you react in a positive or negative way? Do you even have a reaction at all? I can literally breathe deep(exhale) now, but just a minute ago, I was spacing out. It has been more stressful as far as pressure before, but I didn't pay any attention. Let me know what you think! Traci

Tuesday, April 10, 2007

Hoodia works! Lost 20 pounds!
Current mood: accomplished
Category: *Food and Restaurants*

I have taken Hoodia for about a month. I took mine every morning for that amount of time. I lost 20 pounds yay! There were no side effects for me. I drank lots of water. I still do. Now to be truthful I am taking Dexatrim Max. I want to lose 20 more. I will then be satisfied. I will continue to work for PeraltTV, KTVU2, San Leandro and Berkeley School Districts, and attend Laney College for TV Production, and California State University Hayward for my masters in CATESOL. I say this part because people ask me have I exercised to. I say that I have mostly been walking. I have lots of goals to achieve. I say to all women and men who want to lose weight, do what you want to do! Good Luck! Traci

Saturday, April 28, 2007

Final Draft Scriptwriters Showcase! Was it luck!
Current mood: artistic
Category: *Dreams and the Supernatural*

I got a chance to attend the scriptwriters showcase from 4/20-4/22. My friend and I rode AAmtrak, first class on the 19th of April. We then stayed two nights where the showcase conference was being held. I met the CEO of Final Draft. I met Antwone Fisher and gave him two cards of my books, How To Kill A Player and Burnin' From Within. He was the highlight of my trip. The other person Mike Farrah, he works for a company that helps people to get their films made. He asked me to give him my script. Their company helped the guys that made Hustle and Flow. I told him that when I'm done, I will. He said when I was done to call him and let him know. I'm working on it now. I am going to try and go for it. I will still make the movie myself and for the rest of my books. I have been working hard in school to do that. I will continue to work my craft no matter what. I am very glad that I got the chance to go though. It helped me to keep looking towards the future. Traci

Saturday, May 05, 2007

When is there too much weight gone! On crack or not on crack! That is the question(HA HA)
Current mood: exhausted

Don and I have talked about losing too much weight. I told him that I want to be model skinny. I have come to find out that little by little I'm getting smaller. You guys may not even remember when I was in between 135 and 150 was the biggest I would get. I used to do 100 sits in the morning and 100 at night. I was always exercising every night or morning. Truthfully I don't care what yaw think I'm on, I gotta lose weight. I've heard so many people say the word fat behind my back it ain't funny. I look like I've lost some now but I lost twenty and gained it back. All my friends keep saying is you have to go to the gym too. I know it's true because I'm doing all these different things, and I'm losing the weight very slowly. Oh yeah Don and I also talked about people wanting to lose weight, but they still eat up the but. I also found that when i ate just junk for the day, and not even that much it aded more pounds then two meals put together. Yes that's all women talk about! Do I look fat? because to us we know we are. Yes, there's the Black woman thang, but you don't want the weight to kill you! i know it shows a lot more in my arms and face now, that double chin is sort of going away, but I'm working on it. Tell me what you guys think, Let's Talk Traci

Friday, May 18, 2007

Reno/Vegas great trip almost! Traci
Current mood: relieved
Category: *Life*

MY FRIEND AND I WENT TO RENO ON THE 13TH,14TH, AND 15TH. THEN WE WENT TO VEGAS ON THE 14TH,15TH, AND 16TH. WE HAD A GREAT TIME AT THE GRAND SIERRA HOTEL IN RENO. WE ALSO HAD A GOOD TIME AT THE EXCALIBUR HOTEL IN VEGAS. WHEN I WAS IN THE AIRPORT TO GO HOME FROM VEGAS I SPOTTED FRED ENGLISH AND OUR CAMERA MAN GREG. I SPOKE TO THEM AND WAS VERY GLAD TO SEE THEM.

I WAS ABLE TO TAKE PICTURES FOR MY CHANNEL 2 MYSPACE PAGE @ ANCHORKTVU@YAHOO.COM. MY FRIEND TOLD ME THAT HE HAD SPOTTED BILLY BEAN, THE GENERAL MANAGER FROM THE A'S. I AM ALL FOR OAKLAND! LIKE RICKY'S SIGN ON TOP OF RICKY'S SPORTS BAR THEATER AND GRILL, I STILL BELIEVE! LOOK HOW FAR THEY CAME AND WENT! WHEN WE GOT OFF THE PLANE BILLY BEAN WAS GRACIOUS ENOUGH AND NICE ENOUGH, TO GIVE ME HIS AUTOGRAPH! MY FRIEND IS A SPORTS NUT, SO HE TOLD ME ALL ABOUT BILLY BEAN AND THEN CAME OVER TO TALK TO HIM WHILE I WAS GETTING THE AUTOGRAPH. I GOT TO THE AIRPORT AND THE FLIGHT WAS OVER. MY FRIENDS BAG CAME OUT AND MINE DIDN'T! I LEFT A BAGGAGE CLAIM REPORT AT THE SOUTHWEST B.C. DESK AND LEFT! THE NEXT DAY THANKGOODNESS THEY SAID THEY HAD THE BAG AND WOULD BRING IT TO ME THAT MORNING. I WAS HAPPY! I DON'T HAVE MUCH RIGHT NOW, BUT WHAT'S MINE IS MINE! I'M GLAD IT WORKED OUT! TALK TO YOU ALL ON MY NEXT ADVENTURE, TRACI

Friday, June 01, 2007

Lake Camanche
Current mood: chipper
Category: *Travel and Places*

A friend of mine and I went to Lake Camanche for the Memorial day weekend. We went from Friday until Monday. The trip was great but I have to admit, that sun was way too hot. We had to keep finding the shade. The second day we both got on the jet ski for the first time. My friend that I rode with, I hung for about a half an hour. I know it felt like a long time. We went over, all the way, and even though I had on a life jacket I felt like I was drowning. I couldn't breathe for a minute, and I went in far not just a little. Then the Jet ski still had the key in it. My friend told me that it was supposed to come out when you fall off. He had to go and get the jet ski, while I struggled to float. Then the second time we fell over again. He said he did it on purpose the second time. He asked me if I wanted to drive and I said no. He is a great driver though. He is in high school and read to graduate next year. I told him that he should take some of his energy to college, and he said he was going to dvc. On the last day we at least found some shade. Our friends were gracious hosts, there was plenty to eat. My two friends, who are women, did most of the cooking. My other friend did a great job of barbqueing. Oh yeah, our tent was so hot, that we could only sleep in it at night. I want to buy one of my own. It was a great experience! Traci

Thursday, June 07, 2007

Why don't we go to college right after high school! Traci
Current mood: awake
Category: *Goals, Plans, Hopes*

I did not go to college right after high school. I worked for thirteen years before I did. Now I'm going for my masters. I just feel that my life would have been so different, if I had gone right after high school. I would have been a doctor. I would have had a bigger house. I always think my kids would have still been there but only two, or maybe one. I feel that there is more out there to see. I know that you can't change the past. I know I should appreciate what God has given me already. Maybe I should make a film about that. This is my copyright 6/7/07! You all tell me what you feel! Traci

Sunday, June 24, 2007

Why does drama always come into the picture?
Current mood: cold
Category: *Romance and Relationships*

Why is it that adults act like teenagers? They go around saying he say, she say shit. I know that its wrong to blame someone for something they didn't do. Its wrong to use one girl for liking or not liking you, only to make the other girl jealous. Its wrong to be with one girl because she has more money than the other one. Its wrong to be with a hood girl only because you just want to sleep with her. Its not ok to be friends with one girl so she can tell you what all the other girls are like. It's wrong to be with one girl at a club and be with another one the next week. It's wrong to have a babies momma and not acknowledge that you have a kid. Women know a lot of the things that go on with men. We are all grown, but I'm just saying that everyone needs to be careful. Everyone watch your back. We are all supposed to be friends and cordial with each other. You never know who has who to protect them. I take care of myself and I ain't scared! Traci

Tuesday, July 10, 2007

Can women and men just be friends! Yes
Current mood: bitchy
Category: *Friends*

Don and I have been friends for ten years. We have never been intimate with each other. I know what people have heard and said. I am thankful for all of my friends. Let me set the other record straight! I do not nor will I ever sleep with married men. I don't mess with men when I know they have regular women even though the two people may not be married. I'm not the other broad and I'm tired of being accused of it. Most people says that a woman knows when he's with her, but you all know that they will say whatever you want to hear to have that thang with you!

Thursday, July 12, 2007

Happy Birthday Lover!
Current mood: anxious
Category: *Friends*

Last night at Eli's Mile High club we celebrated Lovers Birthday. She looked cute in her baby phat, and her new hair cut. We all had a ball singing and dancing. All her co-workers showed up. Her two brothers were there with their wives. It was full with friends. The phone number is 510-654-4549. They have bands that play on other nights. They have comedy once a month. They have a jam session on Sunday. That is where you all should be. I'm here at Ricky's sports theater bar and grill with Ricky and Tina, typing on my script after keeping up with Myspace. They have karaoke on Friday night. We have a ball too. On Monday night the Serenader by kwik way's at the Lake with Alvon. Everyone make sure that you get out to enjoy all the singing and dancing. I always try to sing and greet people when they come around. I would love to see you guys other places as well. Talk to you soon, Traci!

Saturday, July 14, 2007

Diddy's Assistant! Vote For Me Please! Traci
Current mood: grateful
Category: *Goals, Plans, Hopes*

I spent the whole morning preparing the students at SLHS high for Diddy's Project. I received a bulletin on Myspace from Diddy saying that he needed a personal assistant. When I had the camera out they all wanted to be the camera people. I picked the first two students who raised their hands. One was the camera person, and the other was the director. Then they spent almost an hour talking about it, even though I had passed out their folders for them to do another assignment. I knew they weren't going to want to do anything else, because I was filming. So I had them to participate, and then write a paper on what they would do, if they were able to make the video. Some of them wrote on what they would do if they could work for him. It was hectic but fun! They like to tease me a lot, because they know I'll say something back to them. I have to admit though, they have worked very hard for the first three weeks. Those stacks you see in the video, are just from three weeks of work. My kids are crazy just like me. My friends are to, that's why you see my shirt talking in the end. My friend said," yeah let Diddy see what you got." So I made a crazy one minute video and put it together. I had fun, the students had fun, and I hope Diddy likes it! Please Vote for me at Diddy's Assistant(DiddyAssistant)@ Youtube.com. Your Girl, Traci!

Friday, July 27, 2007

I'm finished with the script! Traci
Current mood: artistic
Category: *Dreams and the Supernatural*

Oh my Gosh It is 4:30p.m. I finished the script(HTKP) at 4:27p.m. today 7-27-07. I am so overjoyed, I had to scream when I was done. I finished it just right, and they could even make a sequel if they needed to. I want to work on the books now. I already paid to have those published I just haven't had the time to type them up. Now I can relax a little, thankyou very much. I will talk to you guys later! Traci

4:25 PM—0 Comments—0 Kudos—Add Comment—Edit—Remove

I'm finished with the script! Traci
Current mood: artistic
Category: *Dreams and the Supernatural*

Oh my Gosh It is 4:30p.m. I finished the script at 4:27p.m. today 7-27-07. I am so overjoyed, I had to scream when I was done. I finished it just right, and they could even make a sequel if they needed to. I want to work on the books now. I already paid to have those published I just haven't had the time to type them up. Now I can relax a little, thankyou very much. I will talk to you guys later! Traci

4:25 PM—0 Comments—0 Kudos—Add Comment—Edit—Remove

Why is it when you go for your goals you feel like your alone?
Current mood: accomplished
Category: *Goals, Plans, Hopes*

Whenever I come up with something new to expand my financial freedom or sanity, I feel like I'm all by myself. I spend a lot of time on this computer now. I have been writing like crazy. I want to invite everyone to come and sing karaoke. They can celebrate with me on August 8th. I want to celebrate because I'm finally done with the movie script. I will send it to Mike Farah, and to Diddy by next week or so. I'm gonna keep trying. I know that people may feel that I'm just talking, but hopefully not for too much longer. I just need to find the right avenue. Then I'm gonna complete my next two books and I'm gonna celebrate again. Traci

Sunday, July 29, 2007

Bobby Billard Is Looking For A Co-Star!
Current mood: artistic
Category: *Art and Photography*

Bobby Billard is looking for a co-star to give her a kiss in The movie, Live Mansion. This is an audition where guys or girls must be professional and very serious about being a star in an actual movie. Please be cordial! This is a regular production! Good Luck to you all.

If you don't have access to a camera use this:

Wednesday, August 01, 2007

Celebrating finishing my movie script!
Current mood: determined
Category: *Dreams and the Supernatural*

Eli's Mile High Club 3629 Mlk. North Oakland May 8th. Next Wednesday! I will be celebrating completing my script. How To Kill A Player. Also being co-producer on another movie, starting work next week! I plan to celebrate finishing my third and fourth books, Die Hard Raider Fans, and Karaok4e In Da Hood. I'm hoping to finish them before the year runs out. Please join me to sing. Traci

Wednesday, August 08, 2007

Come and celebrate tonight! Traci
Current mood: determined
Category: *Dreams and the Supernatural*

Just a reminder! Come to Eli's Mile High Club! I will be celebrating finishing my script and sending it to the Agency in L.A. All I can do is pray and hope that they actually let me have a say in it, or at least work! If they just take it and nothing is done, I will still have to keep going! People say don't wish anything negative on yourself. To me sometimes that's a catch twenty-two. People tell you not to tell people your goals. That's a catch twenty-two too! I always tell my goals because one way or another I'm going to make them happen. If I had the money I would go to Puffy's office and apply in person. I will definitely be able to say that I didn't try! I can actually say now that I am very happy! I have met a lot of my goals. I have worked for channel two,

I have my bachelors degree, and I am going for my masters now. I applied to be Diddy's assistant, I was on the Jenny Jones show, I sent a video in to Oprah for singing. I am a producer on a movie, and worked as a production assistant just last year! One year, you can't beat that promotion, and biggest of all I was karaoke star of the month! I told Diva Dee thanks because no one had ever given me that title before! I thank God for everything that has happened to me within the last few years! I wish you all well in whatever you set your hearts to. Traci

Saturday, August 11, 2007

Come help me! Update Diddy's Assistant Video! Traci
Current mood: anxious
Category: *Goals, Plans, Hopes*

I am going to update my video for Diddy's assistant! Come and help mention why Diddy should hire me! You can just say, Hire Traci if your camera shy! 3629 Martin Luther King, in North Oakland. I will edit it and then put it on youtube.com. This is your chance to be in something, until I finally get there! You know your girl! Always trying new things, Help me out yall! Traci see you next Wednesday August 15th, 2007 at 9. Traci

Monday, August 20, 2007

I'm working on a film! Traci
Current mood: anxious
Category: *Jobs, Work, Careers*

I am associate producer for a film. I am basically calling up the individuals who will be interviewed. They are calling back little by little. It looks as though in September, and October we will be working with cameras. We will be putting together the final product. I will let everyone know when they can look out for the production and what it is all about. Traci

Thursday, August 23, 2007

Diddy's Projects are on myspacetv now! Traci
Current mood: bouncy
Category: *Dreams and the Supernatural*

I have spent the morning uploading my four videos. I am working hard to become Diddy's Personal Assistant! I thank you all for being so great in helping me to get the projects done. I love you all and appreciate the help you have given me sooooooo much! You know that I am karaoke crazy! That's why my friends would call me karaoke queen. Through the countless summers going to karaoke sometimes seven nights a week! I have always wondered about singing all the time for a lot of hours. A few times now I have been hoarse for a few nights and that's why I wasn't singing. I have dreamt about owning a restaurant, and that's why I help out no matter what club I go to. I hope you all enjoy the videos. So far I have had great comments! thank you so much for supporting me with my dreams! I always say, "If you don't go for something you'll never know what happened." I want to try and make it before my brain goes. I wish you all well for whatever you go for! Keep your head up! GodBless! Traci

ALL YOU HAVE TO DO IS CLICK ON VIDEO, ON MY PAGE. THEN CLICK ON WHICH EVER VIDEO YOU WANT TO SEE, OR ALL OF THEM! THEN TO GET BACK TO THE PAGE, CLICK MYSPACE HOME!

Friday, August 24, 2007

Metal Night at Eli's Mile High Club! Traci
Current mood: artistic
Category: *Music*

LAST NIGHT, I SAW FOR THE FIRST TIME FIVE GREAT METAL BANDS. THE BANDS WERE EMBERS, OAKHELM, CHROMIUM SIX, INSATANITY, AND MANIAS. I MET THE GUYS FROM MANIAS WHEN I FIRST GOT TO THE CLUB. THEY WERE REALLY COOL

AND GAVE A GREAT PERFORMANCE. ALL OF THE BANDS WERE GOOD. WHEN YOU GUYS GET THE CHANCE IN A CITY NEAR YOU, OR AT ELI'S MILE HIGH CLUB 3629 MARTIN LUTHER KING JUNIOR ROAD 510-654-4549, OWNER SAM MARSHALL(MARSHALL LAW BAND), COME SEE US! THE NEXT DATE IS AUGUST 30TH @ 9.

Sunday, August 26, 2007

Venus Fly Love! Ladies only night! Traci
Current mood: anxious
Category: *Parties and Nightlife*

Last night was the gathering for venus fly love. Ri and Cynthia are the promoters of the evening. They have house music for everyone to enjoy. The cover is $7. They have a drink that they are promoting called walking on venus, a mixture of malibu passion fruit, bacardi gold, orange juice, and topped with a cherry. The crowd started coming at eleven. It was about 60 plus women who came to party and have fun. A few came in dancing to the music. Some of the women were standing with their friends and talking. They are starting to dance at eleven o four. Bethanie was taking pictures for the evening. The women were all having a ball and it was 12:05. The club was hot fun, and full of people. Kimberly and Treina were there from the Burnin' Bush night. Thomas D. was there to party too. There were people still coming in at 12:41. DiEna was there to party ever since elevenish. Genell was there to party and had come all the way from L.A. The night ended with R playing honey loving kisses by Stevie Wonder. Come to Eli's Mile High Club 3629 Martin Luther King Road, 510-654-4549, and have a good time. They have Jam session on Sunday. They have a blues Band(Billy and the thrillers(Sept.!, !4th, and the 29th), Metal Night(Sept. 30th), and karaoke with myself singing(Wed,thurs, and sometimes Friday). We have a lot of fun at all the events. Most people are cordial, very clean(which is great), and thank you very much for tipping. There are Laura the bar manager, Artenesia, Cathy, and Sam the owner. I am a cosultant/blogger/bar back/security. As usual I have many hats, which I love. I want to own my own bar someday! So come and enjoy, have fun, and just have a great time! Traci

Friday, August 31, 2007

Rock At Eli's Mile High Club! Traci
Current mood: bouncy
Category: *Music*

Dichard Productions Presents IF NOBODY KNEW-WWW.MYSPACE.
COM/IFNOBODYKNEW, THE F-HOLES LOW RED LAND-WWW.
MYSPACE.COM/LOWREDLAND, THE AIMLESS NEVER MISS-WWW.
MYSPACE.COM/THEAIMLESSNEVERMISS, ARE PERFORMING
TONIGHT AT ELI'S MILE HIGH CLUB AT 3629 MARTIN LUTHER
KING ROAD IN NORTH OAKLAND. DOORS OPEN AT EIGHT, 7
BUX. SHOW STARTS AT NINE. 18 AND OVER THANX. Hope you
all come out and enjoy. Eat, drink, and have fun! Traci

6:07 PM—0 Comments—0 Kudos—Add Comment—Edit—Remove

Metal Night at Eli's Mile High Club! Traci
Current mood: awake
Category: *Music*

Last Night the bands were Zeitgeist, Passive Agressive, Valdur, and Elk. The
bands all played very well. They all have very unique styles. Valdur toured all
over northern California and they graced Eli's with their last mini-concert.
Lava Booking/Amanda-Promoter. The bands all play very, very well. When
you get the chance, if you can hang with the black metal sound, come and
visit Eli's. Live music to me is better than anything else. Eli's Mile High Club
3629 Martin Luther King Road, Oakland.CA.

Saturday, September 01, 2007

Blues tonight at Eli's! Traci
Current mood: busy
Category: *Music*

Tonight at Eli's we have Billy and The Thrillers. The cover is ten for the door.
The band is great, and I know because I've seen them perform before. Eli's

has food and drinks for you to purchase! Please come out and eat, drink, and have fun! Traci

5:54 PM—0 Comments—0 Kudos—Add Comment—Edit—Remove

Rock Bands At Eli's! Traci
Current mood: chipper
Category: *Music*

Last night at Eli's there were four bands. Low red Land, The Aimless Never Miss, If Nobody Knew, and F Holes. Again everyone was great! I have a lot of notes for each band. I will make more blogs at a later time. I had a great time again. You cannot beat seeing these bands live. Then helping them out by buying their cd's or t-shirts, like I did. I even received one for free. The bands always need a following! You won't feel disappointed! The people who come to see them are friendly. I like the fact that these people are very intelligent and have great conversations with each other. The bands take time out to do what they love. Music is universal! No matter what your religion is, or if you don't believe in it, come and support the bands! Traci

Monday, September 03, 2007

Youtube! Traci
Current mood: cheerful
Category: *Music*

My youtube site is WWW.YOUTUBE.COM/TGAIN5. WHEN YOU GET THE CHANCE TAKE A LOOK AT MY VIDEOS. THEN LOOK AT ALL THE VIDEOS THAT HAVE INSPIRED ME IN LIFE. TRY SOME OF THE ONES THAT YOU MAY NOT HAVE EVEN HEARD BEFORE! THEY ARE GREAT! I LOVE ALL ARTISTS! TRACI

2:47 PM—0 Comments—0 Kudos—Add Comment—Edit—Remove

New Pics-Screenwriters Conference/L.A. 4-20-4-22-07 Traci
Current mood: artistic
Category: *Goals, Plans, Hopes*

I have finally downloaded the pics from when I went to the screenwriters
conference in April of 07. I had a great time and met Antoine Fisher also. I
met Mike Farah from Southern Cross The Dog, a company where you can
submit a script. I have the date and blogs about the trips and the conference.
I plan on traveling more next year. Traci

Monday, September 10, 2007

Working on my Die Hard Raider Fans! Book, Traci
Current mood: enthralled
Category: *Goals, Plans, Hopes*

I'm sitting here at Ricky's Sports Theater and Grill! I have interviewed a few
people for the book. I will hopefully be finished by the next few months.
RAIDER NATION MAKE SURE THAT YOU CLICK ADD ME AT
WWW.MYSPACE.COM/RAIDERCAT1. I will get prepared soon to write
my next book KARAOKE IN DA HOOD! That's the one everyone says their
waiting on. I hope we win the Superbowl! Go Raiders! I will keep you all
posted on my progress. OF COURSE YOU KNOW I WILL POST THEM
WITH A PIC ON MY PAGE! Good luck to you all in whatever you do. No
matter what, KEEP YOUR HEAD UP ALWAYS! TRACI

Tuesday, September 11, 2007

SUPER HOT NEW AND UNCENSORED CD! TRACI
Current mood: chipper
Category: *Dreams and the Supernatural*

IF YOU WANT THESE LAIDES TO FULFILL YOUR EVERY FANTASY!
IF YOU YOU WANT THESE LADIES TO FULFILL YOUR DEEPEST

DESIRES, SEND 15.99 PLUS FREE SHIPPING AND HANDLING TO GIRLS TELL ALL PO BOX 7730 LAKELAND,FLORIDA(FA) 33807-7730. IF YOU GET THE CHANCE TO USE YOUR CREDIT CARD AND YOU WANT TO PURCHASE THE CD RIGHT AWAY, GO TO WWW.GIRLSTELLITALL.COM FOR MORE INFO. HAVE A GREAT TIME, AND PLEASURE TRACI

4:49 PM—0 Comments—0 Kudos—Add Comment—Edit—Remove

KIMBALL'S CARNIVAL TONIGHT! TRACI
Category: *Music*

COME AND ENJOY! KIMBALL'S HAS A DRESS CODE,SUITS, AND DRESSY CASUAL. I BELIEVE THERE IS A NO TENNIS SHOES,BOOTS,AND TEE-SHIRT RULE! MAKE SURE YOU HAVE YOUR ID'S! COME EAT,DRINK,AND HAVE FUN WITH VERN(KJ). I HAVE KNOWN VERN FOR A LONG TIME NOW, AND HE IS GREAT WHEN IT COMES TO KARAOKE! SEE YOU GUYS THERE AT ABOUT EIGHT THIRTY/NINE! TRACI

4:19 PM—0 Comments—0 Kudos—Add Comment—Edit—Remove

CLICK STORYTELLER!MYSPACETV.COM TRACI
Current mood: bouncy
Category: *Dreams and the Supernatural*

I JUST ENETERED THE CONTEST FOR A NEW SHOW ON FOX! I DOWNLOADED MY VIDEO TO BE DIDDY'S PERSONAL ASSISTANT! YOU ALL KNOW YOU WANT TO DO THIS! CLICK OM STORRY TELLER WHEN YOU GO TO MY PAGE, WWW.MYSPACE.COM/TRACIGAINES CLICK ON VIDEOS! CLICK ON STORYTELLER! THEY SAY THEY WILL CHOOSE FROM THE ONES THAT THE PEOPLE VOTE ON. HELP ME IN MAKING THIS THE NEXT,ON HIT, REALITY TV SHOW! TRACI GAINES EVERYONE REMEMBER,KEEP YOUR HEAD UP, AND DO WELL IN WHATEVER YOU WANT TO DO! TRACI

3:34 AM—0 Comments—0 Kudos—Add Comment—Edit—Remove

APARTMENT C! VERY NICE, CHECK IT OUT! TRACI
Current mood: cheerful
Category: *Music*

I HAD THE CHANCE TO GO AND SEE ONE OF OUR FAVORITE KJ'S, PUMPKIN AT APARTMENT C. THE PLACE LOOKS REALLY NICE. WE HAD A LOT OF FUN. IT WILL BE ON MONDAYS'. THEY HAVE GREAT FOOD FOR YOU TO EAT. COME EAT, DRINK, AND HAVE FUN! TRACI

Friday, September 21, 2007

Diddy's Unforgivable Party Is Hot, Very Hot! Traci
Current mood: chipper
Category: *Music*

I was just able to place Diddy's Unforgivable party on my page! The party is hot, and my question was asked! B5 cd coming out! They look like they were all having a ball including the Hosts from 106 and Park and Diddy's Artist! Take a look! Also his commercial was shown at 2:22am on MTV HOT HOT HOT! TRACI

2:25 AM—0 Comments—0 Kudos—Add Comment—Edit—Remove

Wednesday, September 19, 2007

PRIVIES NEEDS YOUR VOTE! TRACI
Current mood: creative
Category: *Music*

THEY ARE IN THE BATTLE OF THE BANDS AND NEED YOUR VOTE! YOU CAN VOTE AT WWW.NEWBODOGBATTLE.COM/BANDMUSIC/178688/PRIVIES TO VOTE. I HOPE ALL IS GOING WELL FOR EVERYONE OUT THERE! KEEP YOUR HEAD UP! TRACI

6:51 AM—0 Comments—0 Kudos—Add Comment—Edit—Remove

Sunday, September 16, 2007

BOMANI,KHE NOTES, AND RAISED BAI ROBOTS! TRACI
Current mood: anxious
Category: *Music*

OH MY GOD WHAT A GREAT NIGHT! KHELA FROM KHE NOTES BAND(BAND LEADER/SONGWRITER EXTROIDANAIRE/ VOCALIST) SANG HER BEHIND OFF! HER SOUND IS UNIQUE. THE SONGS ARE ORIGINALS. SHE SANG TWO COVERS, BUT SHE DID THEM JUSTICE. BOMANI-ATIIM(BAND LEADER/SPOKEN WORD PROFESSIONAL), BECCA(PROFESSIONAL DANCE HIP HOP/BALLERINA), KHELA(VOCALIST/RAP ARTIST), THE FIVE OTHER GREAT MEMBERS ARE GREAT! THEY HAD A JAZ/HIP HOP/ R AND B SOUND THAT BLEW ME AWAY. BECCA DANCED WHILE ATTIM SPOKE, AND ATTIM'A ENERGY IS GREAT, HE CAN DANCE AND LEAD THE BAND ALL AT THE SAME TIME! ONE WOMEN PLAYED THE FLUTE AND THE SAX, SHE WAS WONDERFUL. ONE WOMAN PLAYED THE CONGAS, AND THE CHIMES. THE PERCUSSIONIST AND THE GUITARISTS WHERE WONDERFUL AND VERY SKILLED. RAISEDBAIROBOTS HAD THREE BAND MEMBERS. THE BAND LEADER SAID THAT THEY PLAY A SORT OF MYSTERIOUS INDIE ROCK WITH CONCIOUSNESS MIXED IN. THEY HAD A LOT OF ENERGY. THEY PLAYED A LOT OF SONGS, AND EVEN SOME FOR THE ENCORE. THEY HAVE T'S FOR SALE TEN BUCKS, IF YOU GET THE CHANCE TO SEE THEM. COME OUT AND SUPPORT BOMANI MUSIC EVERY 3RD SATURDAY, COVER IS TEN. EAT, DRINK,AND, ENJOY! TRACI

10:18 AM—0 Comments—0 Kudos—Add Comment—Edit—Remove

Saturday, September 15, 2007

ELI'S MILE HIGH CLUB!BOMANI TONIGHT REGGAE LAST NIGHT! TRACI
Current mood: amused
Category: *Music*

LAST NIGHT ADIGGAJAMS PRESENTED CARRIBEAN SPICE AND EVOLUTION. THEY WERE BOTH GREAT REGGAE BANDS. JADIGGA AVONI AND BLAZE NOVA ARE THE PROMOTERS. LAURA(MANAGER),CATHY(BARTENDER), AND SAM(OWNER) WERE THERE TO GRRET EVERYONE. I HAVE HEARD RAVE REVIEWS ABOUT THE ATTITUDES OF YOUR HOSTS, AND IT HAS BEEN GREAT! TONIGHT IS THE GROUP BOMANI. IT'S FROM 8-1:00P.M. 3629 MARTIN LUTHER KING JR. Way (NORTH)OAKLAND. COVER IS 10.

4:49 PM—0 Comments—0 Kudos—Add Comment—Edit—Remove

Thursday, September 13, 2007

Ricky's Sports Grill and Steakhouse! Traci 9/16 & 17 Sat.&Sun.
Current mood: chipper
Category: *Sports*

COME EAT AT THE BUFFET! THE COST IS 18.95 FOR ALL YOU CAN EAT! 15028 HESPERIAN BLVD. SAN LEANDRO (510) 352-0200, WWW.RICKY'S.COM. Also on the menu they have the main events choices. They have the steakhouse specials. They have Ricky's hall of fame sandwiches. They have Ricky's game day burgers. I recommend the Ricky's Buger, or try all of them. They have the pre-game appetizers. They have lots to drink and eat! Eat, drink, and enjoy! Traci

www.ingramcontent.com/pod-product-compliance
Lightning Source LLC
Chambersburg PA
CBHW031328290526
45784CB00014B/2415